Hi, my name is Asa. I am A hardcore
And in this book, I am going to be gu   ₂
a prayer warrior very first step is understanding who god is, God is your
helper, your healer, your best friend of all time, and he wants to be able
to speak to you Now how do you start to talk to God? That takes us to
step 2, opening your heart to Jesus. I will be helping you get

closer to God, but The first thing I want you to do is to pray this short
brand with me! Father God, in the name of Jesus, I come before you,
invite you into my life, and wash me clean of all my sins. In Jesus' name,
we pray amen The next thing you need to do is open up to him, even if
it's just moving "hi God, how are you doing today" I want to encourage
you to open up to God because no matter what you are going through,
a friend, the loss of a loved one, or Divorce; whatever the case may be,
I want to

encourage you to open up to God Now, let me Prayer on a trip back to
when I Was young. I started playing baseball doing WCBMX, was invited
To a few Special events, met a few celebrities, Cities in a magazine,
been on the news, been in a commercial, and maybe I thought, okay
now, he's just bragging. I'm not bragging. I am telling you to know.
What Has been doing this for me. Moving on to the present You may be
thinking, well, what else has What has God done for Him? Well, believe
it or not, I have had

two back-to-back surgeries on my back, which contours, But That is not
my only surgery. I Have Had sixteen surgical procedures on me, which
probably got you thinking about how I am Alive and well. I answer that
question with a single word, god; the answer might think god has much
for you, Asa; what can he do for The what can he do me? Well, I shall
be too. The question is actually in the Bible. In the scripture, ask

anything, in my Name and shall Be Done. It will not be instantly done because he does not

Work on our time, not our time but believe me when I Say that he will support you. Maybe you are in a relationship that feels like the perfect relationship, but you End up I was breaking up. Well, there's an ideal reason for that, Which Is That god has another person in mind can; Some of you may find yourself, well, I'm a little skeptical about w. Still, I am reading and thinking to This can't be true; everything

I have said it is true, but I will tell you it will not be easy. You will still have what I like to call roadblocks But Remember that with god, anything is possible now; it may sound skeptical, but Let me tell you. Something he will reveal himself in the most mysterious ways. For example, he could show himself in a dream and reveal Thoughts. Now You might ask me, do I connect with him regularly? Well, have you made him a part of Your life? If you have not, I will help you all receive him, father, in the name of Jesus; I repent of all my sins; please wash me clean of all my sins. I open my heart and my Soul To you. I make you the lord of my life. In the name of Jesus, we pray amen and amen, so what has the Lord done one or you? Maybe he brought you a girlfriend/wife or boyfriend/husband. It c? There is the pet you've wanted. It could be a brother or a sister, whatever the case might be; just know he wants to bless you every day. Do we know how he is going to bless us? No, but I will tell you this he has blessed me. Remember, and if he's blessed me, then I can assure you that he will bless you. Something

Remember Bible mentions is t god will only forgive seventy-seven times now. Am I saying that we are perfect? No, we all have errors that can be improved but not perfectly But that's what makes us all unique, so the next time someone says, "why can't you be perfect like me, perfecexcellents don't fight? Instead, with a person, they communicate well; god made me who I am, and it is just OK With me,

Him. Don't let the devil bring you down; instead, listen to excellent about; God will; h a way of no way. Let's say, like me, you have a disability and got bullied for it. Well, does god want you to be driven away because of what you have and are going through? No, but we are all being tested on our faith in god. My

goal is to help you get as close as possible to pass the test; there are three parts to the test of faith understanding and instruction. Following now, you might think, what does he mare threshing? The education I am talking about is in the Bible; thou Shall not kill, steal or destroy. These are just a few of gods commandments in the Bible, but there are more than can Be found in the Bible. Now I understand if you find this book very dull but trust me, at the end of this book, you will have learned more about what god can do and how to get closer to him. If you are still confused after reading this book, I will

leave some contact information so you can get ahold But back To The teaching, see, there's no limit to what god can Do for You. I mean, I had A twenty-minute seizure that scared me, so I was rushed to the emergency room; of course, before the attack, I had been coughing well; I was afraid I was going to miss

my graduation, which was the following day I prayed to God that I would be out of the emergency room, and god answered my prayers I was out of the emergency room by midnight well, I was happy because I was able to make my graduation, and I rolled across the stage saying, thank you, Jesus, it's a miracle but don't get me wrong I've had numerous attacks from the devil like the Seizures I mentioned, but the devil has tried multiple times to distract me from god, but he has failed every time he has tried to attack me I've been left behind in a fire drill when I was in grade school, well as you can probably imagine It gave Me severe post-traumatic Stress disorder, short PTSD, for years, but I overcame it with the power of god. I even asked if there going to be a fire drill where is the fire extinguisher but fast forwarding again to March fifth of 2022 I became an ordained minister, but at the age of 13, I became a storm spotter,

who's very hard to do. I've been a storm spotter since elementary school, so it was tough to manage both going to school and being a storm spotter, but I love both the jobs I do but again, enough about me. It's time to focus on yourself and how you feel, mentally and physically. If you feel like you Have a problem in or on those areas, then your room or somewhere private and ask god to help you. Now I will prophesy something over you and your family, a reversal of whatever you are going through. I pray that

you and your family get through it in the name of Jesus; I want you to know how much god loves you. He loves you so much that he sent his only begotten son to die for us on the cross. He took unimaginable beatings for us when he died on that cross. It is said that the word Bible stands for basic instruction before leaving earth al And he also said that he would be whatever you need him to be, whether it is protected. He said I would be whatever you need to be, but again he wants to become

closer to you and talk To you more and bless you abundantly, open your hearts to him and let him live inside you. I promise you excellent and unimaginable things will happen to you if you allow him to live inside of you, but you have to learn to build up your faith, then talk to him, tell him how you feel, and he will help you, for example

, the woman with the issue of blood who said if I could touch the bottom of his clothes, I shall be healed, but it wasn't the clothes that healed her, but it was her faith that healed her god has made the blind see

Isn't that amazing if he can do all that then is there anything he can't do well to answer that question no there isn't anything he can't do

So what can he do for you well he can do anything you want him to do and he will be anything you need him to be now are there certain things you shouldn't say oh absolutely

and those words include the f bomb

The word hell but there's an exemption with this word you can use only in a prayer

The word shit

The d word

Now do those words slip out of our mouths sometimes yes but we must try to avoid these words now you might be thinking ok now he is controlling our life

Well I'm not like I had said before I am only trying to help you

Now the only other thing I can guide you too is to pick up that Bible but another thing we need to remember is communion

Now you might be asking well what is communion well it's also known as the lords last meal

Now you are asking well why is this very important well we do this in remembrance of what he did for us

But all of gods instructions can be found throughout the Bible

Okay you may be getting annoyed with me but don't worry I'm almost done then I'll leave you alone

Now some of you might be like "no I want more" well if you are tired of reading this then there are plenty more Christian authors out in the world who happen to be Christians like myself now I'm going to take a break here for a moment just to ask how you think god can help you? Well I mean if he can do all those things for me he can definitely do amazing things for you in your life

Another thing that god wants us to do is to go out and lay hands on the sick and pray for them and another thing god wants us to do is to spread his words to other people that is what he wants us to do

Just bare with me a little bit longer and I promise I will be quiet lol but I want to say a lot more before I actually be quiet and stop nagging at you lol but let me tell you soSSomething god will make a way out of no way

What do I mean by that? You would probably think a paraplegic like myself would have trouble cooking or cleaning. Now there's a ton of stuff I have problems with, like reaching high oobjects or surfaces

But that does not stop me because I know For a fact that if god is with me, nothing is impossible, and nothing by any means can harm me according to the word of god

I was able to prophesy over my family members thanks to God being with me and in me; what I said yesterday was, "FOR GOD HAS SAID THE TIME OF DESTRUCTION IS OVER FOR NOW IS THE TIME OF REST AND RESTORATION FOR I HAVE COME DOWN ON THIS EARTH TO SET THINGS RIGHT, AND FOR I HAVE COME DOWN TO HEAL YOU, FOR THE DEVIL HAS BEEN DEFEATED AND BOUND IN HEVAN, AND YOUR

HEALING HAS BEEN LOOSED UPON YOU." I woke up this morning to check on my family, and they told me they were no Longer. Wouldn't you agree with the power of god that did that, or what would you think about it? All of the miracles I've mentioned so far are just the tip of the iceberg; my dear friend, when god died on the cross of Calvary, he took our curses, our sorrow, our pain, our diseases, and our iniquities it may sound skeptical to A lot of you but everything I have said is the 100 percent truth now to Make things a But more fun; I will List a few songs that will encourage you to learn the word of god

One of the songs Is the way maker, another piece is blessed the lord oh my soul, and many more, so if you're into Reading, then I hope you've found my book helpful, but if reading isn't your cup of tea, then I would recommend listening to Ebooks,

but it's ultimately up to you. I can't tell you what to do, and I do not want to say to you what you have to do. I don't control your life you do, So whatever is your Cup of tea, read or listen to an ebook, then do what is right for you to learn

As this is my first book, it may not make sense to all of you, which is why I told you I would leave my social media available at the end of this book

so if you still have questions about something in this book, you can reach out to me 24/7 because I would love to be able to communicate with my audience, even if you want to start a general conversation that isn't about the book like I said to reach out because again I want to be able to greet you

I hope this book has taught you everything you need to know about how to get closer to god and communicate with him and more about what he can do through What I've taught you from my life story

If you want to learn about what else god loves or about what the devil hates, then keep an eye out for my next book entitled what god loves and what the devil hates, but I will go ahead and teach you just a little bit about that

see, the devil hates when you speak In the heavenly la; hege, he hates when you give God the praise, honor, and glory he deserves. Let's say you are going through a dark Time but do not fret because god will be your light in the darkness, and as I mentioned earlier, he will be your way maker, your miracles worker, but what he wants the most is to be closer to you

See, he wants us to listen to his voice because when he speaks to all of us, He's guiding us on the path he wants us to be on.

Remember, he wants to bless you and your family and friends

But that ,comes when you invite him into your heart but, most importantly, into your own home. Now he is in you, but he is waiting to talk to you

As I mentioned a while ago, it can just start as a general hi, how are you doing today god

And just let it go from there, and soon you'll be talking to god in no time

Now with all of that out of the way, take a minute to reflect on what you have learned so far from this book, and I promise I'm almost done with just a couple more pages to go

But my dear friend, if you are going through anything and you need to seek some help, my advice to you is always to go to god first. He will have the answers to what you are seeking or going through. He always has the answers

Remember that god loves you and will never leave you or forsake (abandon) you because even before you were born, god was with you, and even after you were born, he has never left you

If you need someone that is available to talk to you day and night; call on god because he is ready to speak to you no matter the time or the day ,or the year

Now my primary mission for the rest of the book is to try and inspire you to talk, seek, and of course, follow him because once you start following him, and you've made him the lord of your life; supernatural things will start happening to you

And Who knows, it might even affect your life forever because god only wants the best for his children, which includes you, the reader of the book, but don't be scared of the sudden change in your life because it's gods work!

But how will you know he's working on and in you, well you have to believe in him and trust me when I say that you will be highly appreciative of his works, so look out for a positive impact on your life that will change your view on life

Now I want to remind you how much god loves you because his love for you is endless

With all of that being said I am happy to inform you that we will be closing soon but before we do close there are a few more thing's I want to talk about in this book

Now yes you'll still have people that will hate you but that's gods way of telling you hey these people aren't really your friends they are just acting as your friends but do not worry god has the perfect set of friends for you

But something I have not touched on is speaking in the holy language which to some people may just sound like complete gibberish well when you pray in tongues you are actually driving the devil out because he does not understand what you are saying however god does understand

And here is another example of things that god can do to help you one major thing we all are dealing or have been dealing with which is addictions rather the addiction be drugs alcohol smoking cussing or it might be an online addiction

Whatever the case may be just know god is there to help you steer away from the addiction now once you are out of the addiction you must repent the only addiction you must have is an addiction to the word of God

Like for instance my dad recently got out of an alcoholic addiction so did my godfather which is a blessing from God

If you are in an abusive relationship ask God to help you out of that relationship if you are pregnant and the doctor is saying your baby won't make it through birth go to god don't be upset because God will make sure that your little bundle of joy will make it past birth and god will make sure that your newborn baby is happy healthy and whole

It wasn't until July 5th of 2022 I decided to become an ordained minister and I am still an ordained minister to this day now am I telling you to become an ordained minister or a storm spotter absolutely not

What I am telling you is the amazing things god has done for me and he's also done incredible things for my family in fact I receive a lot of prayer requests which I am going to be praying over you and your family

My friend No matter what you are going through just know I am here to help you but most importantly that god is always there for you so if you are in pain cast it to the pit of hell if you have anxiety cast it to the pit of hell or whatever attacks the devil is trying to put against you cast it to the pit of hell

You have the power to make the devil run away from you as scriptures say if God is with you therefore who can be against you

Now as promised here are the ways you can contact me

Snapchat Asag6131

Tiktok Skywarnspotter93953

Email Asag613@yahoo.com

But back to what I was saying how can you make the devil run away from you or your friends or family simple answer is by prayer but a real way to send him running and crying is the power of tongues

Now I have a new question for you the reader and that question is what would you rather have torture in hell or blessings from heaven because god said with long life shall I satisfy you and show you my salvation

Now you might be busy with school or work but never draw away from God

What has god blessed you with today? Was it a new car a new job a new house whatever the case may be god is always wanting to bless you

so what is the biggest blessing you've been given whatever it is remember to give god praise honor and glory for it and a more than desirable outcome is for sure going to happen to you

It has been a real honor for me to get to have taught you today now I know I've been extremely repetitive not because I'm running out of things to say but because I want to make sure I'm getting everything through to you

but I am actually very curious about what the biggest blessing you've received is maybe its one of the examples I gave or it maybe something else but whatever it is I want to hear from you about what it was and how you have been using it and if you want to get even closer to God then I'll be more than happy to help you with that

Okay now lets talk about ALL of the benefits of praying which are praise reports now you might be asking me well Asa what does a praise report sound like well I've had a few praise reports What were they you might be asking (or you may be frustrated at me for not being quiet like I said I would a million times already)

BUT a praise report for example one of the praise reports I've received was from a friend of mine when I was 12 years of age and I remember what he said

He said "Asa thank you for taking the time out of your day to help me with my addiction problem the day after you had prayed for me I had been cleared of my drug addiction) I was in my room saying to myself THANK YOU LORD

Now did It happen right away no it happened a few months after I had prayed over him another report I received was only a few days ago that my dad had cut back on his alcoholic beverages see what I mean both of the examples I gave you shows the goodness of God

Now I'm going to ask you something and please be honest about it but what has god done for you that classifies as a praise reports maybe it's one of the example's I gave you today or it could be something I have not mentioned but I would like to hear from you about what it was

And your like well what do I need to do to receive praise reports well again the answer is in the Bible which says lay hands on the sick and they shall be made well.

and if you're into online dating like I used to be then I'm telling you don't do that because again god will send you a perfect girlfriend or boyfriend which in the Bible is called a help mate

Now the power of tongues and prayers are EXTREMELY important but not only are they important but they are also EXTREMELY POWERFUL if you learn to speak in tongues or pray in the name of Jesus then a desirable outcome is indeed expected.

And this one may seem more unbelievable than the other examples that I had given to you earlier about what Jesus can do

He can calm a harsh storm you can find that story in Matthew chapter 8 verses 23 through 27

It can also be found In

Mark 4 verses 35 through 41

And finally Luke 8 verses 22 through 25

There are multiple chapters and verses that speaks about what God can do for you it starts with the line in the beginning god created the heavens and the earth in the story of the ARK of Noah Jesus was able to calm the harsh waters

Isn't that awesome! Well the greatest act of love that he did for all of us on this earth as I mentioned earlier is that he sent his only begotten son to die for us on the cross of Calvary.

but he didn't do that and said okay my work here is done no he did other things such as go to hell for us but he beat the devil and took his keys but when he was crucified (killed) on that cross he rose from the grave on the third day

So my brothers and sisters in Christ if you are dealing with a sickness or a family emergency just know that god has your back 100 percent of the way As pastor John Hagee said

If you don't forgive, you're imprisoned by the offense. Set yourself free by choosing to forgive! Meaning if someone did something bad to you and you haven't forgiven them then you are still choosing to follow the devil Instead of forgiving those who have done wrong against you as God wants you to forgive and forget and just to focus on him God's word CAN NOT RETURN VOID (or as a lie for those who don't know what void means in that context)

Now the next thing I want to talk about is distractions the devil will try to make you pay more attention to him by trying to distract you and make you move away from god examples of distractions include your phone going off countless times or maybe you need your phone for work but keep getting distracted by annoying ads that's just a few of the ways that the devil will try to distract you.

But please remember that your main focus needs to be on god if you lose focus on him then you are letting the devil steal your opportunity for living the life that you want to live but if you follow the devil you'll be living a life of pain sorrow regret and so on and so forth so my new question for you is would you rather live the life that god wants you to live or live the life that the devil wants you to live

Well I hope you choose the life God wants you to live but I would like the opportunity to pray for you once again father in the name of your son Jesus Christ I pray for the person reading this book father I COMMAND THE CHAIN'S AND THE ROADBLOCKS IN THIS INDIVIDUALS LIFE TO BE BROKEN IN THE NAME OF JESUS devil I say to you that your plans will never work you're a defeated foe and in the name of Jesus I CAST YOU OUT AND SAY GET YOUR HANDS OFF OF GOD'S CHILDREN in Jesus name we pray amen and amen

Now repeat after me god I loose the power of healing over my life and my friends and my family in the name of God And devil I CAST YOU BACK TO THE PIT OF HELL FROM WHICH YOU CAME I decree and declare that the attacks you throw at me shall have no effect on my life in the name of Jesus

Remember the Bible says whatever you loose in earth shall be loosed in heaven and whatever you bind on earth shall be bound in heaven now I trust that you will take this teaching in your heart and soul and use it to make your life better and more blessed and have entrusted your life to God.

Now if you're struggling with an assignment or with work then stop take a minute to breathe and ask god to help you do whatever it is that you need too get done

Another thing is lets say there's a tornado or a snowstorm that is heading directly for you ask god to provide you with protection.

How do you do that exactly Well in the word of God it says "for I will place a hedge of thorny protection upon you

What I'm try to say to you is that god will be whatever you need or want him to be for example he will be your guardian if you need him to be and whatever else you might need him to be he will be.

I know I've said this many times but please never forget that god is with you loving you and that he will never leave you or forsake you because he is a good God who cares for all his children day and night week after week month after month year after year (well you get the idea lol) he's always with you.

Now what I want you to do is grab a pen or a pencil and a few pieces of paper and write down all that god has done for you and when you have a rough day or are beginning to feel very discouraged I want you to look at those pieces of paper and begin to thank God and ask him for forgiveness and to bring you back on his path.

Now I understand that we all mess up from time to time and god understands so if we make a little accident or whatever god is willing to forgive you and help you get back on track.

See how wonderful God is now the most important thing is false images of God so if you see an image of him that looms really pretty or whatnot that is indeed a false image of God but if you want a real image of what god looks like well get into that Bible because the images you are seeing now in the bible are considered graven images .

What do I mean by graven images well in other words I mean you are receiving false images of God which is another thing the devil will try to attack you with is indeed false image of God now what else does the devil try to attack you with well I went over some examples bit other examples of the devils attacks are addictions and of course lies and deception.

However as I said earlier god is an honest god I may not finish all my teaching in this one book and that is okay it just means there might be a part two but as I was saying are we all perfect people absolutely not (if I hurt your feelings saying that then indeed I apologize because that was not my intention at all) but we can train ourselves to be better by following the word of God and not only the word of God but also his instructions.

Like I said the Bible is always the way to go because again the word Bible is not only gods book but again Bible also stands for basic instruction before leaving earth and if you follow his instructions and praise worship and honor him for what he has done for you but be very careful about what you say because if you say something like oh I'm sick and I'm going to die that's worshiping the devil as my friend says you can't serve two masters you can either love one and hate the other and vise versa so if your parents or other adults say be careful what you say please listen to them

So instead of saying oh yeah I'm sick say oh no I'm not sick not at all I feel great glory to God

And if someone says hey you need to see the doctor or hey you need to go to the hospital/emergency room in that case tell that individual hey you know I already have a doctor who is available every minute of every day and is always with me and that doctor is doctor Jesus

Isn't that amazing that god is always there for you no matter what and that he wants to bless us abundantly beyond what we could imagine and guess what the blessings are ready for us to accept them all we have to do is accept it and say okay this is the blessing that God prepared especially for me and now I thank you God for this blessing and I will happily accept this blessing you have prepared for me.

And if people start to judge you for believing on god just look them in the eye and say you know what if that's what you think about me than that's fine but I was made in God's image.

Now again I'm not by any means telling you what to do or how to live your life but rather I am trying to help you get closer to god and we are all gods children and we were all made in his image so instead of saying oh yeah I'm okay say well I don't know about you but boy did I wake up blessed this morning.

Are you enjoying this teaching so far if so tell me what was your favorite part of the book and let me know if you want me to keep writing more books but what did you learn from this book did it inspire you did it make you look at life.

No matter what god has done for you remember to give him praise even if its just for waking up this morning remember our God is 3 in one now you might be asking well how can he be three in one well he's the father the son and the holy spirit.

Remember we are all children of the most high god who's name is above all names remember when the doctor's say that you need to take medicine to get better that's the devil talking to you just say no I have my medicine already which that medicine is indeed the word of God

Okay now I am going to tell you what to do (lol) when you feel sick then just say devil I rebuke you in the name of Jesus

Once you go on the path of God so much joy love and of course laughter is to follow trust me it will be a very noticeable change in your life. Like just a few days ago (months or years ago by the time you read this I actually got a girlfriend.

See what god can do he always has the desire to keep you healthy happy and whole isn't that amazing see I even made a prophecy and that prophecy was that there will be a great reversal on this earth debt will be reversed sicknesses will be reversed family emergencies will be reversed and gone.

See you may not realize it but when you pray or prophecy over someone that's god using you as his vessel to spread his word to others now again there will be some tests that will be thrown at you like for example scammers trying to take all your money it's all just a test to see how big your faith in God is.

Now I'm trying to help you all pass the test but again all the answer's you need for life are in the Bible which is why I strongly encourage you to read the Bible and feed on God's word until the word of God gets in your heart.

See all of this I have learned as a Christian being in a wheelchair but I know that I still have a lot of things to learn but I'll get that done eventually I just have to take it day by day and remember what god told me to do while I'm on this earth and yet I also still have to learn how I can improve myself.

Now again will I be able to improve my self until I am perfect absolutely not but you know that's okay because I will never want to change who god made me to be even though people try to bring me down I always tell myself if God is with me than who can be against me and he also said that no weapon that is formed against me shall prosper.

And I've been living by those two biblical quotes ever since I first started reading the Bible which was a long time ago but I have god and his word deep inside my heart remember this your real friends are the ones who encourage you to get out of the mess you are in.

Also remember

Stay on the direct route by listening to the voice of God every day and giving Him thanks

God isn't out to punish you. Actually, He went out of His way by sending His son Jesus to die just to free you from the chains of sin and shame.

These are quotes from a few pastors that I don't know personally but have seen on television I have met a pastor in my life though but I guess what I'm trying to say here is that our god is absolutely wonderful and he loves each and every person on this planet.

But again we have to remember to give him all the praise the honor and the glory he deserves like I've had 16 surgical procedures done on me and my first surgery when I was two years old and I'm still here on this planet at 19 almost 20 years old (probably older by the time this book is published).

if you are still with me thank you but if you quit I understand because I've been yapping and yapping at you lol but just hang in there for a little while longer but I promise you that I'll try to stop yapping at you as soon as I am finished here.

Now I know we're all super busy with work or school or planning things but please take time out of your busy schedule to spend some time with our awesome god and create a deep connection and friendship with him.

Now let's say someone comes up to you and says oh you're extremely ugly or oh you're so fat you look like a bowling ball don't let that get to you because that's the devil talking and trying to ruin your day and make you feel insecure about yourself.

So at anytime this happens to you just remember god made you in his image and god will love you no matter how you feel or look isn't that amazing that he loves us all no matter what and here's a quote from pastor John Hagee.

You must totally forgive the person or persons that hurt you. Release them! The moment you do, you are the one that walks out of the prison you've been in!

See the Bible says forgive and you shall be forgiven have you been in a situation that you felt like it would be impossible to get out of well let God intervene because God will make a way out of no way and if you are in a dark place do not worry call on god.

So again what has God done for you now back to the subject of addiction there's plenty of things

You can become addicted to like medicine for example people try to kill themselves by overdosing or for short OD

Now personally have I done that no because that's of the devil

I truly believe that God is going to bless you abundantly above all that you could have ever asked for now all of God's blessings can be yours of you have the faith of a mustard seed but of course we all want that seed of faith to grow as big as it possibly can right?

Well in order to do that you have to feed your mind body and soul the word of God then you have to believe in him and his words

Remember how I said online dating is a no well that's because the person you are in a relationship with is not the person who god intended you to be with patients my dear friend and trust me God will send you the perfect person to be with for the rest of your life.

Like it took many years until God sent me the person he wanted me to be with and honestly I could not be any happier than I am right now.

Okay on to something else see people often ask me hey Asa how do you deal with paralysis and seizures and I tell them well that is a question with a very simple answer which is I have god on my side all the time.

That is how I deal with everything is just going to the lord who always has the answers to everything

Here's another quote from Jesse Duplantis

When you walk closely with God, you'll see it's time to stop looking back at the old & step into the NEW! It's time to say goodbye to limitations & setbacks. Expect old hindrances to be removed & doors of opportunity to swing open! It's time to soar into a new season of blessing! Do you claim that new season of blessings because I know I sure do.

but do you claim that new season of blessings why or why not? I know most of you are like "OK ASA SHUT UP ALREADY "but honestly there's lots more I want to cover like the spirit of fear for example some of that fear could be from a doctor's report or a bad dream or memory.

What are some things that cause you fear or worry? Well luckily there's an exercise which is the same one we went over a few page's ago so again what I want you to do is grab a few more pieces of paper and write fear or worry on those pieces of paper on them and then just STOMP ON THOSE PAPERS

Then just say out loud these ate now under my feet

Now you might be asking man he's been talking about feet a lot does he have an addiction with feet to answer your question no I do not so let me take some time here to explain the significance of the word feet and why I keeping mentioning the word feet (you can skip this section of the book if you want but I feel like it's very important for us to understand the significance of the word feet)

see when Jesus went down to hell he put the devil under his feet and took the keys of hell that's why I kept mentioning the word feet so if Jesus can put the devil under his feet then so can we now you might be asking me how and well again the answer too that question is indeed prayer!

Now the power of tongues and the power of prayer are super powerful and should not be used incorrectly just like how I prayed for my friends Jimmy and Emily which when you pray over someone god is using you as his vessel.

What other supernatural stuff can god do

He can walk on water he can turn water into wine and MUCH MORE!

Now me I'm such a weather geek so when it rains I know it's god pouring out his blessings upon all of us in the world in fact there are 47 Bible scriptures that talks about the significance of the weather you are witnessing today in fact even the seasons we all witness are in the Bible too!

Now you may be asking me well Asa why are you mentioning this well what if someone has a fear of storms like I did as a child and the lord had spoken to me today 2/24/23 and said fear not my child for this rain is not being sent to harm you for it has been sent to rain my blessings down across the world.

We have all seen lightning /thunder in storms but what exactly does thunder signify in the Bible well rge significance of lightning/thunder is a sign of God's presence on the earth isn't that amazing that god reveals himself in ways we would never expect him to

Now those here in Texas rarely see this event but what about snow what is the significance of that weather event well the significance of that is forgiveness of sin

See how cool the Bible is it can teach us stuff we didn't know now let's talk about numbers (I know again very random) but the cross that Jesus died on for us actually represents the number 3

Now we always hear people tell us not to say the numbers 666 why well because that number represents the UNHOLY trinity.

it is extremely important to understand the significance of numbers in the Bible now some people may tell you oh the Bible isn't a real book or that Jesus isn't real do not believe them because they are trying to get you away from the path God wants you to be on

and if you believe that person then start realizing that you are on the wrong path then all you have to do is get on your knees and repent to god about what you did wrong and ask him to forgive you again and lead you back to the path you need to be on.

Now am I trying to call you out on stuff you did wrong no not one bit but if I did accidentally call you out for something that you did do wrong I apologize

I also prayed over my friend Maye because she wasn't feeling well (for personal reasons I will not mention what was wrong) but a few weeks later she texted me again and said that she was feeling much better.

Do you have someone in your family who is sick If that is the case what I want you to do is visit them and just say a quick prayer for that family member rather it be your mom your dad your brother or your sister just say a quick little prayer for that person because God said if you lay hands on the sick they shall be healed.

If you do all of this your life will be changed forever and I mean a supernatural change in your life will take place Just like it has for me.

Have you noticed anything that was or is different about life now well that's god that's working in you

What I'm trying to say is that God's word is always helpful and it's instructions on how to keep living the life that god wants you to live part of that life he wants you to live requires you to remember what he did for you by taking the last supper Also known as communion but I will say this that communion can also be a curse if you take it unworthily

In other words we have to make sure we ate worthy of the lords communion or if we are unworthy

Have you ever been in a bad car accident and were okay well that's god protecting you from any harm because the Bible says that whatever the devil meant to use evilly against you the lord will turn it into a blessing and the Bible also mentions the lord saying that nothing by any means can harm you.

So get ready for those praise reports to come in to you and you will be witnessing the goodness of God very soon and you might be able to hear him speak to you which is a real blessing the blessings you receive may even be to the point you need a journal to write all of the blessings down.

The reason I mention this is because I believe that God is going to overflow your life with abundant blessings even more than you can think of not just because he loves you but he wants you to live the best life you can ever think about living.

Well do you want all of that of course you do well the first step to receiving the lord into your life

And trust me what God is going to do for you is going to make you say wow but not a disappointment kind of way but in a blessed kind of way. Now I might be boring you and I apologize for that.

So what have you been blessed with in your life and how do you plan to use those blessings don't just throw them away because you're avoiding the life god wants you to be living

Are you feeling weak today well start repeating the scripture the joy of the lord is my strength and keep repeating that scripture to yourself every day and every night until its drilled into your mind.

The reason I'm telling you this is because the more the word of God is drilled in your head the more your life will change

I know this was supposed to be about my life as a Christian in a wheelchair but I decided to change it into a teaching because I want to help and encourage you the best that I can but I will definitely keep teaching you as long as the lord tells me to keep writing these teaching books.

Which leads me to a new question which would be have you ever partaken in communion or the last supper if so did you feel like it has changed you if so then how

Don't let anyone or anything stop you from being a follower of the lord instead just say through god all things are possible or you could say lord you are my way maker and I need a way to get out of this situation show me how you want me to do this lord.

He will show you the way when you feel like there is no way out of the situation you are currently in all you have to do is call upon the name of the lord and he will guild you out of that situation.

You might be saying well Asa my life has been absolutely horrible and I'm starting to feel like there is no hope left in my life its always going to be horrible don't say that because you just glorified the devil Instead glorify the lord by asking him to renew your hope and repent of what you previously said.

There are multiple versions of the Bible which are all worded differently but remember even though the Bible you may have is worded now you may want to notice on the Bible the names Luke john Peter so on and so forth those are the names of the individuals that wrote that specific book in the Bible.

Remember The blessing of God is available to whosoever will believe it & put it to work!

Now there's so much more that the Bible has to teach us in fact this one book didn't even cover half of what the Bible teaches us but moving on to spending as much time as possible with God rather if it's at lunch after dinner or if you're home sick just read spend time with God and I'd encourage you to try to spend at least a little over an hour with him every day or more time than that if you can.

Now on to the subject of timing in the Bible 3 P.M is actually very significant remember how I kept going on and on and on about how Jesus died on the cross of Calvary well time actually ties in with his crucifixion on the cross of Calvary why does time tie in with his crucifixion you may ask well because 3 P.M was the time that Jesus died for us

But he died from the most brutal beating you could ever imagine he was beaten his arms were nailed on that cross but I think you may know the story behind that or at least have a pretty good idea of what he was going through when he got brutally beaten before he died on the cross for more on that story it can be found in mark chapter fifteen verses 37 through 39.

I mean that just shows us how great our God is doesn't it I mean he gave up his sons life just so that we could be happy healthy and whole I mean giving up God's only begotten son for us to me that sounds like an unbelievable act of love don't you think?

I mean there's absolutely no reason not to worship and praise God just remember psalms 105:1

"Oh, give thanks to the Lord, Call upon His name; Make known His deeds among the peoples!"

Do you plan to use the information that is in this book if so how do you plan to use the information or if you don't plan to use the information that's in this book why not

But its ultimately your decision if you want to make him the lord of your life I can't force you to do anything I can only encourage you to do it but I hope this book has been able to encourage you to make him the lord of your life.

Remember never let the devil get to you or try to get control over you by using an addiction against you which he could pull you in by using a money addiction or by putting incorrect words in your mouth when you're praying.

Which is why I am trying to encourage you to make god the lord of your life because otherwise the devil will try and trick you by dressing up as an angle but he always gives himself away by lying.

There's something else I want you to remember which is god rewards faithfulness even in the little things also remember "But seek ye first the kingdom of God, and his righteousness; and all these things shall be added unto you."

And one more thing to remember seek the lord and you shall find the answers to any questions you may have for him

Well how do I know I've connected with God well the most common way is belief and faith and he will reveal himself with visions or a dream in fact there are multiple ways that he can reveal himself which can indeed be the weather.

Has god revealed himself to you if so how

I want to prophecy over you and your family that god will reveal himself to you in a very unexpected way and that he will bless you abundantly in Jesus name Amen and Amen now as Mr. Joel Osteen said

You have to be willing to accept the new things God is going to do. His dream for your life is much bigger than your own. Where God is going to take you, the doors He's going to open, the people you're going to meet, it's going to be more than you ever imagined.

Which was what most of this book was actually about accepting god into your life and accepting the new blessings that he has prepared especially for you do you accept that blessing that he's prepared just for you.

Now back on the subject of weather and how god can reveal himself to you well today 1/24/23 we had multiple tornado warnings and multiple tornado touch downs pretty much all day but the amazing thing is that nobody got hurt

See like I said god will reveal himself in ways that even we do not see coming and back to the subject of addiction one final time I know you guys ate probably yelling at me saying "STOP REPEATING SUBJECTS YOU ALREADY TOUCHED ON MULTIPLE TIMES "

Now what else do I have to say about addiction before I finally be quiet with you all On this subject well there's more than just online addictions like for example the addiction of sugar well there are plenty of things that you can be addicted to.

Online or offline addiction is a serious problem which can lead to self harm which is what the devil wants to do is to harm you

Okay finally shutting up completely about addiction and let's go on back to the subject of protection there are multiple times throughout the day we need to be protected such as at school or at work or in the mall

Which is where the 91st psalm comes in because the 91st psalm is the prayer of protection which we need to say that prayer every day but believe it or not god is always with us protecting us day and night every day

Isn't that amazing that god knows what we need before we even ask for it and I know I've asked a lot of questions in this book as well and I apologize for being so talkative even though I've said multiple times now that I would shut up and stop yapping and picking on you all

But again I'm just trying to help you get closer to the lord and to help you understand how to grasp on the wonderful blessings that god has to give you and here's another quote I want all of you to remember

The problem is not with who you are; it's with what you can see. If you're going to reach your potential, you have to constantly clear out things that are hindering your vision.

Now MR. Joel Osteen isn't talking about physical vision but he's talking about spiritual vision like the ability to see god himself or his angels

Now on the subject of money. Money can be a blessing but it can also be seen as a curse. What exactly do I mean by that well if you have a love of money then that's a curse but if you have money and you tithe your money to god then he will return the favor by multiplying the amount you gave to him back to you.

But I'm not going to shut up quite yet because there's still so much to learn in fact this book may not even cover everything there is to still be learned

In fact I have a question for you all which would be do you believe in God or not id you don't then why not

Now it is my absolute pleasure to pray for you regardless of what your request of prayer is I want to be able to pray over you so it doesn't matter if you leave your request in a review or if you leave your request on my social media I want to be able to pray for you and be able to connect with you.

But I got a lot more stuff to cover like scriptures of what he did for us now for this part I'm leaving the scriptures and what Jesus did for us according these 97 scriptures the first one is John 3:16 which talks about him giving up his only begotten son. According to the following quoted scripture

"For God so loved the world, that he gave his only Son, that whoever believes in him should not perish but have eternal life. That's john 3:16-17

Now there are a few of these scriptures that I have not mentioned that will be listed as well such as the following scripture

Titus 3:5

He saved us, not because of works done by us in righteousness, but according to his own mercy, by the washing of regeneration and renewal of the Holy Spirit,

Ephesians 2:8-9

For by grace you have been saved through faith. And this is not your own doing; it is the gift of God, not a result of works, so that no one may boast.

Revelations 4:11

"Worthy are you, our Lord and God, to receive glory and honor and power, for you created all things, and by your will they existed and were created."

Hebrews 11:6

And without faith it is impossible to please him, for whoever would draw near to God must believe that he exists and that he rewards those who seek him

Romans 5:8

But God shows his love for us in that while we were still sinners, Christ died for us.

John 20:17

Jesus said to her, "Do not cling to me, for I have not yet ascended to the Father; but go to my brothers and say to them, 'I am ascending to my Father and your Father, to my God and your God.'"

John 4:24

God is spirit, and those who worship him must worship in spirit and truth."

Revelations 1:8

"I am the Alpha and the Omega," says the Lord God, "who is and who was and who is to come, the Almighty.

1st Timothy 1:17

To the King of the ages, immortal, invisible, the only God, be honor and glory forever and ever. Amen.

Acts 3:19

Repent therefore, and turn back, that your sins may be blotted out,

John 1:3

All things were made through him, and without him was not any thing made that was made.

Luke 15:7

Just so, I tell you, there will be more joy in heaven over one sinner who repents than over ninety-nine righteous persons who need no repentance.

Matthew 23:9

And call no man your father on earth, for you have one Father, who is in heaven.

Ecclesiastes 12:7

And the dust returns to the earth as it was, and the spirit returns to God who gave it.

Job 10:8

Your hands fashioned and made me, and now you have destroyed me altogether.

Revelations 4:8

And the four living creatures, each of them with six wings, are full of eyes all around and within, and day and night they never cease to say, "Holy, holy, holy, is the Lord God Almighty, who was and is and is to come!"

Revelations 1:5

And from Jesus Christ the faithful witness, the firstborn of the dead, and the ruler of kings on earth. To him who loves us and has freed us from our sins by his blood

Jude 1:25

To the only God, our Savior, through Jesus Christ our Lord, be glory, majesty, dominion, and authority, before all time and now and forever. Amen.

1st john 5:7

For there are three that testify:

1st Peter 1:20

He was foreknown before the foundation of the world but was made manifest in the last times for the sake of you

1st peter 1:17

And if you call on him as Father who judges impartially according to each one's deeds, conduct yourselves with fear throughout the time of your exile,

James 2:19

You believe that God is one; you do well. Even the demons believe—and shudder!

James 1:17

Every good gift and every perfect gift is from above, coming down from the Father of lights, with whom there is no variation or shadow due to change.

Hebrews 10:17

Then he adds, "I will remember their sins and their lawless deeds no more."

Hebrews 3:4

(For every house is built by someone, but the builder of all things is God.)

2 Timothy 3:16

All Scripture is breathed out by God and profitable for teaching, for reproof, for correction, and for training in righteousness,

Colossians 1:15

He is the image of the invisible God, the firstborn of all creation.

Philippians 2:2

Complete my joy by being of the same mind, having the same love, being in full accord and of one mind.

Ephesians 4:6

One God and Father of all, who is over all and through all and in all.

Ephesians 4:2

With all humility and gentleness, with patience, bearing with one another in love,

Ephesians 1:20

That he worked in Christ when he raised him from the dead and seated him at his right hand in the heavenly places,

Galatians 5:19-26

Now the works of the flesh are evident: sexual immorality, impurity, sensuality, idolatry, sorcery, enmity, strife, jealousy, fits of anger, rivalries, dissensions, divisions, envy, drunkenness, orgies, and things like these. I warn you, as I warned you before, that those who do such things will not inherit the kingdom of God. But the fruit of the Spirit is love, joy, peace, patience, kindness, goodness, faithfulness, gentleness, self-control; against such things there is no law. ...

Galatians 2:20

I have been crucified with Christ. It is no longer I who live, but Christ who lives in me. And the life I now live in the flesh I live by faith in the Son of God, who loved me and gave himself for me.

1st Corinthians 13:12

For now we see in a mirror dimly, but then face to face. Now I know in part; then I shall know fully, even as I have been fully known.

1s Corinthians 10:31

So, whether you eat or drink, or whatever you do, do all to the glory of God

1st Corinthians 8:6

Yet for us there is one God, the Father, from whom are all things and for whom we exist, and one Lord, Jesus Christ, through whom are all things and through whom we exist.

1st Corinthians 8:4

Therefore, as to the eating of food offered to idols, we know that "an idol has no real existence," and that "there is no God but one."

Romans 10:9

Because, if you confess with your mouth that Jesus is Lord and believe in your heart that God raised him from the dead, you will be saved.

Romans 8:37-39

No, in all these things we are more than conquerors through him who loved us. For I am sure that neither death nor life, nor angels nor rulers, nor things present nor things to come, nor powers, nor height nor depth, nor anything else in all creation, will be able to separate us from the love of God in Christ Jesus our Lord.

Romans 8:28

And we know that for those who love God all things work together for good, for those who are called according to his purpose.

Romans 3:1-31

Then what advantage has the Jew? Or what is the value of circumcision? Much in every way. To begin with, the Jews were entrusted with the oracles of God. What if some were unfaithful? Does their faithlessness nullify the faithfulness of God? By no means! Let God be true though every one were a liar, as it is written, "That you may be justified in your words, and prevail when you are judged." But if our unrighteousness serves to show the righteousness of God, what shall we say? That God is unrighteous to inflict wrath on us? (I speak in a human way.) ...

Romans 2:4

Or do you presume on the riches of his kindness and forbearance and patience, not knowing that God's kindness is meant to lead you to repentance?

Romans 1:20

For his invisible attributes, namely, his eternal power and divine nature, have been clearly perceived, ever since the creation of the world, in the things that have been made. So they are without excuse.

Acts 17:30-31

The times of ignorance God overlooked, but now he commands all people everywhere to repent, because he has fixed a day on which he will judge the world in righteousness by a man whom he has appointed; and of this he has given assurance to all by raising him from the dead."

Acts 16:31

And they said, "Believe in the Lord Jesus, and you will be saved, you and your household."

Acts 14:15

Men, why are you doing these things? We also are men, of like nature with you, and we bring you good news, that you should turn from these vain things to a living God, who made the heaven and the earth and the sea and all that is in them.

Acts 10:34

So Peter opened his mouth and said: "Truly I understand that God shows no partiality,

Acts 9:1-9

But Saul, still breathing threats and murder against the disciples of the Lord, went to the high priest and asked him for letters to the synagogues at Damascus, so that if he found any belonging to the Way, men or women, he might bring them bound to Jerusalem. Now as he went on his way, he approached Damascus, and suddenly a light from heaven shone around him. And falling to the ground, he heard a voice saying to him, "Saul, Saul, why are you persecuting me?" And he said, "Who are you, Lord?" And he said, "I am Jesus, whom you are persecuting. …

Acts 2:38

And Peter said to them, "Repent and be baptized every one of you in the name of Jesus Christ for the forgiveness of your sins, and you will receive the gift of the Holy Spirit

John 17:23

I in them and you in me, that they may become perfectly one, so that the world may know that you sent me and loved them even as you loved me.

John 13:34-35

A new commandment I give to you, that you love one another: just as I have loved you, you also are to love one another. By this all people will know that you are my disciples, if you have love for one another."

John 10:30

I and the Father are one."

John 5:25-29

"Truly, truly, I say to you, an hour is coming, and is now here, when the dead will hear the voice of the Son of God, and those who hear will live. For as the Father has life in himself, so he has granted the Son also to have life in himself. And he has given him authority to execute judgment, because he is the Son of Man. Do not marvel at this, for an hour is coming when all who are in the tombs will hear his voice and come out, those who have done good to the resurrection of life, and those who have done evil to the resurrection of judgment.

John 5:24

Truly, truly, I say to you, whoever hears my word and believes him who sent me has eternal life. He does not come into judgment, but has passed from death to life.

John 3:36

Whoever believes in the Son has eternal life; whoever does not obey the Son shall not see life, but the wrath of God remains on him.

John 3:17

For God did not send his Son into the world to condemn the world, but in order that the world might be saved through him.

John 3:14-21

And as Moses lifted up the serpent in the wilderness, so must the Son of Man be lifted up, that whoever believes in him may have eternal life. "For God so loved the world, that he gave his only Son, that whoever believes in him should not perish but have eternal life. For God did not send his Son into the world to condemn the world, but in order that the world might be saved through him. Whoever believes in him is not condemned, but whoever does not believe is condemned already, because he has not believed in the name of the only Son of God. ...

John 1:18

No one has ever seen God; the only God, who is at the Father's side, he has made him known.

John 1:14

And the Word became flesh and dwelt among us, and we have seen his glory, glory as of the only Son from the Father, full of grace and truth.

John 1:12-13

But to all who did receive him, who believed in his name, he gave the right to become children of God, who were born, not of blood nor of the will of the flesh nor of the will of man, but of God.

John 1:1-51

In the beginning was the Word, and the Word was with God, and the Word was God. He was in the beginning with God. All things were made through him, and without him was not any thing made that was made. In him was life, and the life was the light of men. The light shines in the darkness, and the darkness has not overcome it. ...

John 1:1

In the beginning was the Word, and the Word was with God, and the Word was God.

Luke 21:1-4

Jesus looked up and saw the rich putting their gifts into the offering box, and he saw a poor widow put in two small copper coins. And he said, "Truly, I tell you, this poor widow has put in more than all of them. For they all contributed out of their abundance, but she out of her poverty put in all she had to live on."

Mark 12:28-30

And one of the scribes came up and heard them disputing with one another, and seeing that he answered them well, asked him, "Which commandment is the most important of all?" Jesus answered, "The most important is, 'Hear, O Israel: The Lord our God, the Lord is one. And you shall love the Lord your God with all your heart and with all your soul and with all your mind and with all your strength.

Matthew 28:19

Go therefore and make disciples of all nations, baptizing them in the name of the Father and of the Son and of the Holy Spirit

Matthew 25:31-46

When the Son of Man comes in his glory, and all the angels with him, then he will sit on his glorious throne. Before him will be gathered all the nations, and he will separate people one from another as a shepherd separates the sheep from the goats. And he will place the sheep on his right, but the goats on the left. Then the King will say to those on his right, 'Come, you who are blessed by my Father, inherit the kingdom prepared for you from the foundation of the world. For I was hungry and you gave me food, I was thirsty and you gave me drink, I was a stranger and you welcomed me, ...

Matthew 7:11

If you then, who are evil, know how to give good gifts to your children, how much more will your Father who is in heaven give good things to those who ask him!

Mathew 7:1-29

"Judge not, that you be not judged. For with the judgment you pronounce you will be judged, and with the measure you use it will be measured to you. Why do you see the speck that is in your brother's eye, but do not notice the log that is in your own eye? Or how can you say to your brother, 'Let me take the speck out of your eye,' when there is the log in your own eye? You hypocrite, first take the log out of your own eye, and then you will see clearly to take the speck out of your brother's eye. …

Now I know you're probably thinking oh my gosh Asa shut up already well I can't shut up yet but shortly after this page I promise you that I will be quiet (putting that in from time to time for the fun of it)

Matthew 5:43-48

You have heard that it was said, 'You shall love your neighbor and hate your enemy.' But I say to you, Love your enemies and pray for those who persecute you, so that you may be sons of your Father who is in heaven. For he makes his sun rise on the evil and on the good, and sends rain on the just and on the unjust. For if you love those who love you, what reward do you have? Do not even the tax collectors do the same? And if you greet only your brothers, what more are you doing than others? Do not even the Gentiles do the same? …

Matthew 5:16

In the same way, let your light shine before others, so that they may see your good works and give glory to your Father who is in heaven.

Well you get the idea but see isn't god really amazing he did all of this for us but there is one more scripture I want to share with you before we wrap this book up which that scripture would be

Numbers 21:4-9

From Mount Hor they set out by the way to the Red Sea, to go around the land of Edom. And the people became impatient on the way. And the people spoke against God and against Moses, "Why have you brought us up out of Egypt to die in the wilderness? For there is no food and no water, and we loathe this worthless food." Then the Lord sent fiery serpents among the people, and they bit the people, so that many people of Israel died. And the people came to Moses and said, "We have sinned, for we have spoken against the Lord and against you. Pray to the Lord, that he take away the serpents from us." So Moses prayed for the people. And the Lord said to Moses, "Make a fiery serpent and set it on a pole, and everyone who is bitten, when he sees it, shall live." ...

Have you ever had an encounter with Jesus if so where did you encounter him was it from a dream or a vision?

I know I've asked you a lot of questions but I as your friend and the author want to be able to connect with you

So the next time you have a storm in your area make it a holy storm by looking at the following scriptures such as Isiah 4:6 which quotes the following :

It will be a shelter and shade from the heat of the day, and a refuge and hiding place from the storm and rain.

Luke 2:52

And Jesus grew in wisdom and stature, and in favor with God and man.

Matthew 8:26

He replied, "You of little faith, why are you so afraid?" Then he got up and rebuked the winds and the waves, and it was completely calm.

Nahum 1:7

The LORD is good, a refuge in times of trouble. He cares for those who trust in him,

Psalms 107:29

He stilled the storm to a whisper; the waves of the sea were hushed.

Psalms 119:105

Your word is a lamp for my feet, a light on my path.

Roman's 15:4

For everything that was written in the past was written to teach us, so that through the endurance taught in the Scriptures and the encouragement they provide we might have hope.

Sorry I know a lot of scriptures given today but I want to make sure the word of God is drilled in your head

Well that's all I have for you this is ordained minister Asa saying have a great day and god bless you all and remember that god is absolutely good

CPSIA information can be obtained
at www.ICGtesting.com
Printed in the USA
LVHW061101190323
741893LV00057B/1580

9 789356 753648